IMAGINE ART

IMAGINE ART

Henry D. Wingfield

CITI OF
BOOKS

CITIOFBOOKS, INC.
3736 Eubank NE Suite A1
Albuquerque, NM 87111-3579
www.citiofbooks.com

Hotline : 1 (877) 389-2759
Fax :   1 (505) 930-7244

Ordering Information:

Quantity sales. Special discounts are available on quantity purchases by corporations, associations, and others. For details, contact the publisher at the address above.

Printed in the United States of America.

ISBN-13:	Paperback	979-8-89391-877-9
	eBook	979-8-89391-878-6

Library of Congress Control Number: 2025917281

MY HELP

My Pappy always said, "Hank, give credit where credit is due."

So I would like to thank my pappy and my mother, too. And my two brothers for all the adventures we explored growing, and for sharing their growing families with me now.

And, lastly, thanks to you, dear reader, for sharing these very personal visions of yours. You are the artist.

MY CONCEPT

I cannot draw with any skill or accuracy, and my abstract painting comes out a sheer mess. But I still need you to see the images in my mind, as if you were being swept away by a dream.

So I ask you to look beyond these blank pages to create within your mind the images suggested by visionary words, like a sorcerer conjuring up a potion. Each of you will see a different picture. I have left blank pages, so that if you wish, you may enter your own drawings.

This is an empty book full of visions, dreams, and suggestions. With the power of your imagination, you may create from it infinite artwork.

May your imagination never fade, for when it does, our picture of life begins to fade, as this book will fade. I pray this never happens, for without our imagination, we are nothing.

So I leave it to you. Mix the colors and images of my words, and create your own masterpieces . . . you are the artist.

Acres and acres of six foot sunflowers on a hot summer day in Kansas

Conservatory rose garden in a glass greenhouse—
nothing but blossoms as far as the eye can see

A California vineyard—rows of grapevines, miles long, leading down to the sea

Black walnuts scattered on the ground under a walnut tree in an open grassy pasture

Three twelve year old boys, swimming in a
sun-dappled pond, splashing each other

A swaying footbridge, spanning a deep chasm, far below is a raging river

Three pandas, sitting and nibbling on tender shoots in a lush bamboo forest

A beaver's dam made of logs, river overflowing

Electric guitars leaning on stage scaffolding beside a drum kit—
in the background, rolling farmland

A rickety model-T chugging down a dirt road,
dogs chasing it

The rising sun bursting from behind the peaks of a
snowcapped, jagged mountain range

A man and a woman, back to back in a canoe, floating on a lake, casting fishing lines .... no other people around

A bowl of fruit on a wooden table in a rustic cottage kitchen— fluttering window curtains, a rock wall outside, sheep in the pasture

A fat dill pickle—woman biting into it, mouth puckering

A crowded sidewalk café—people sipping coffee, talking, gesturing—umbrellas at full spoke

Festival in a small Mexican village—mariachis playing, dancers swirling in bright costumes, banners flying from balconies

Amazon River natives on the river bank flinging fish nets

Eskimo family laughing and talking as they dry their hides
on a wooden rack

Ripples on a pond, an osprey skimming the water with a rainbow trout in its talons

A family of orangutans high in a tree, grooming each other

A pair of raccoons washing their paws

A stumbling baby giraffe taking its first steps,
mother close by

A boy strolling through a golden meadow, tackle box in hand, fishing pole over his shoulder

A Mexican sombrero on a sandy beach next to a row boat

A steamy Japanese bath house,—beautiful tile work,
flower arrangements

A wild landscape of geysers and hot springs,
steam swirling in a wind

A Zen rock garden in a Buddhist monastery, boulders and
stones portraying waves in the sand

A pretty Chinese peasant woman, water buckets balanced on a pole over her shoulders, walking down a dusty dirt road

Sunset glistening on the ocean, a tall ship in full sail,
tacking out of a rocky harbor

Frosty night—a coal-black sky, dazzling sparkling stars

A railroad crack leading into a tunnel through a mountain,
you can see light of day at the other end

A fishing boat, swaying with the ocean swells— a lobsterman
leans over a splintered rail, hauling up a lobster trap

An old, unshaven man in a rocking chair, dozing in the sun

Three tee-pees in an open meadow on the bank of a river,
horses tied to trees, fire pits in front of each tee-pee

A rustic English village, thatch cottages, a horse and cart on
a rutted road

A tuba lying alone on a sun-beaten barren desert,
a scorpion in its shadow

The sun setting fast, like a fireball drowning in the sea

An artist at her easel in a New York City loft, a vase of flowers on a stool—three attic windows propped open

The eye of a needle

A kid swinging on a monkey vine over a lake

An archer standing with full drawn bow aiming at a target leaning on a tripod

A blue ball balanced on top of a green bottle

A parade passing through Time Square . . . .
confetti floating from the tall buildings

A child riding on a brightly painted carousel pony

Three kites flying high in the air, three kids in a park
holding the spools of string

Japanese garden with pagoda and an arched bridge
spanning the pond

One butterfly lighting on a tulip

A swamp-like bog, cattails and reeds,
cypress trees and a rowboat tied to a dock

A desert with saguaro cactus, mountains in the background
and ravens flying overhead

A major boulevard downtown in a big city

Campers siting around a campfire, tents in the background

A butterfly lighting on a blossom, a bee buzzing nearby

A man fishing from the end of a dock

Candles burning in a candelabra

A hot air ballon, hovering 2 feet off the ground
with a name printed on it

A lighthouse on the point of a canal entering a harbor,
a boar coming into port

Crescent moon, starry night

A scarecrow standing in a cornfield,
a bird perched on its arm

A child flying a kite in a field

A totem pole with eagle wings at the top

A castle surrounded by a moat, drawbridge opening

A snowman

Flag flying at half-mast, a lone gravesite

An apple with a worm and wormhole

The 18th green of a golf course, three golf balls

A football field

A rock balanced on cop of another

A windmill and tulips

Cows in a pasture, one big oak tree in the middle of the field

Three pyramids next to the Sphinx

A ladder leaning against an adobe home

Glass vase full of long stem roses sitting on a table top

A waterfall cascading through a narrow crevice of a cliff

A Christmas tree with packages under it, a rocking horse

A giraffe

A winding road, no cars, roadside hedges and trees

A big blooming flower

Rain clouds, lightning bolts and rain

An airplane flying over an island with a person stranded on it;
one palm tree, "HELP" written in the sand

A pond with ripples showing where a pebble had been
thrown

Ink well in a desk, feather quill and a paper on top

A beach, its surf, a rock jetty,
and a fisherman casting from the last rock

A grizzly bear pawing at salmon in the river

A grandfather clock next to a coat rack, a table, a mirror, and an umbrella stand

Puffy clouds filling the sky; a small cottage with a walkway

A brick fireplace with a mantle and a portrait hanging above

Two people paddling a canoe

People of every color, laughing together

Imagine yourself, a self-portrait—how do you see yourself?

Imagine Art

www.ingramcontent.com/pod-product-compliance
Lightning Source LLC
Chambersburg PA
CBHW051225120626
46547CB00013B/1514